SCHIRMER'S LIBRARY
OF MUSICAL CLASSICS

Vol. 1869

ERIK SATIE

Three Gymnopedies

For the Piano

Edited by

JOSEPH PROSTAKOFF

ISBN 978-0-7935-2590-4

G. SCHIRMER, Inc.

DISTRIBUTED BY

HAL•LEONARD®
CORPORATION
7777 W. BLUEMOUND RD. P.O. BOX 13819 MILWAUKEE, WI 53213

à Mademoiselle Jeanne de Bret

Three Gymnopedies*

Edited by Joseph Prostakoff

Erik Satie

1

* Ceremonial choral dances performed at ancient Greek festivals.

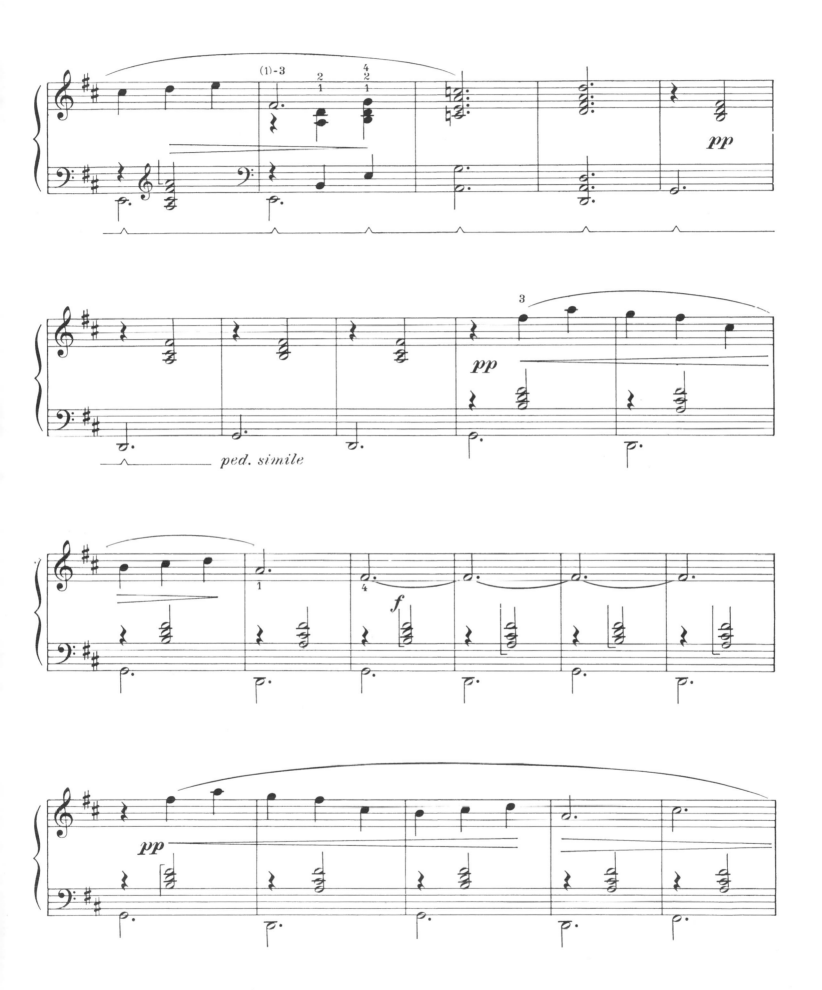

à Conrad Satie

2

Lent et triste (slowly and sadly)

à Charles Levade

3

Lent et grave (slowly and solemnly)